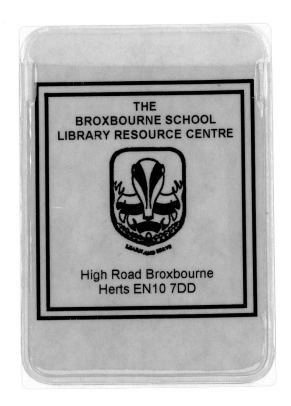

THE
BROXBOURNE SCHOOL
LIBRARY RESOURCE CENTRE

High Road Broxbourne
Herts EN10 7DD

ISSUES IN OUR WORLD

CHINA
The New Superpower

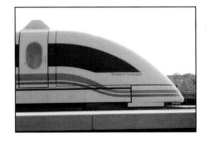

Antony Mason

Aladdin / Watts
London • Sydney

ABOUT THIS BOOK

China is developing fast into one of the world's greatest industrial nations. This is a major achievement for a country that had to rise out of poverty. This book explores how these changes came about and whether China can become the next superpower.

© Aladdin Books Ltd 2009

Designed and produced by Aladdin Books Ltd
PO Box 53987
London SW15 2SF

ISBN 978 0 7496 8631 4

First published in 2009
by Franklin Watts
338 Euston Road
London NW1 3BH

Franklin Watts Australia
Level 17/207 Kent Street
Sydney NSW 2000

Franklin Watts is a division of Hachette Children's Books,
an Hachette Livre UK company.
www.hachettelivre.co.uk

A CIP record for this book is available from
the British Library

Dewey Classification: 951.06

Printed in Malaysia

Designers: Pete Bennett – PBD;
Flick, Book Design and Graphics
Editor: Katie Harker, Vivian Foster
Picture Research: Harker & Bennett
Editorial consultant: Professor Peter Preston, Department of
Political Science and International Studies, University of
Birmingham, UK.

The author
Antony Mason is a freelance editor and author of more than
60 books for both children and adults.

CONTENTS

INTRODUCTION

Look around you. There is probably something made in China close at hand – a pencil, a calculator, a toy. Over the last 25 years, China has turned into one of the world's largest manufacturers. In the 1970s, China was an impoverished Third-World country, so how did it turn itself around?

Commuters cycle into China's capital city, Beijing.

THE GIANT AWAKENS

With 1.3 billion people, China has the largest population in the world. This means that one in every five human beings is Chinese.

One of the most advanced and sophisticated civilisations on Earth, China's history can be traced back at least 4,000 years. But the last two centuries have been deeply troubled. The Communist government created a destitute population who were scared of the police state. To the outside world, China was a mysterious country. All this changed in the 1970s, when the government changed its policies.

China attracted world traders by making products at a fraction of the price charged by other countries. It also attracted international industries with their new ideas.

RAPID CHANGE

Since then, the cities of China have grown at an amazing rate, encouraging a new generation of young, well-educated and ambitious people.

This rapid change has come at a cost, as the gap between the rich and poor widens. China is trying to prove that it has what it takes to become a superpower.

2008 Olympic Games

The 2008 Olympic Games were held in Beijing. China was eager to demonstrate to the rest of the world their new and stylish ways, and spent more than $100 billion on their sports facilities.

Work included building ultra-modern stadiums. China not only wanted to host a brilliant Games, it also wanted to come out top in the medal league. With 3,000 special sports schools training champions of the future, China's athletes will play a big part in years to come.

5

Shanghai – China's largest city and financial capital – is bristling with ultra-modern buildings. However, many residents are still living in poverty.

China's cities and provinces

China has 32 cities with a population of over a million. About 400 million Chinese live in cities while 900 million live in the rural areas. The ten largest cities are outlined below.

Shanghai 9 million
Beijing (Peking) 7.1 million
Tianjin (Tientsin) 4.3 million
Wuhan (Hankow) 4 million
Shenyang 3.5 million
Guangzhou (Canton) 3.4 million
Nanjing 2.8 million
Harbin 2.7 million

Xian 2.6 million
Chongqing (Chungking) 2.3 million

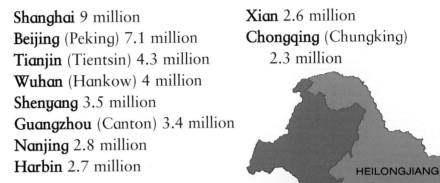

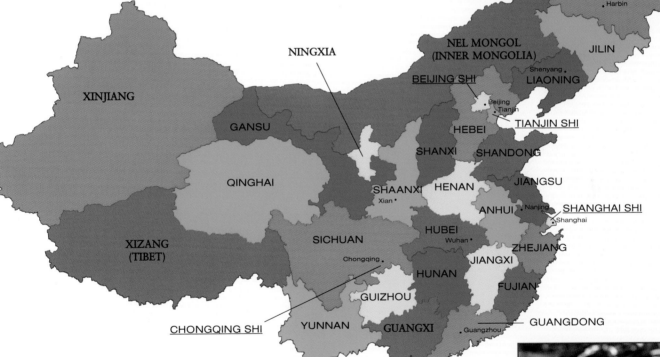

China is divided into 22 provinces plus 5 autonomous regions (shown in bold) and 4 municipalities (shown underlined).

Full name: The People's Republic of China (PRC)
Capital: Beijing
Population: 1.3 billion
Land area: 9,651,000 sq km
Language: Mandarin (92 per cent of the population), Cantonese, Wu, Hakka and hundreds of dialects (but the written language is the same for all).
Currency: Renminbi ('People's Currency'), in which 1 yuan is divided into 100 fen.

8

The Chinese language

Chinese written words look very different to those of other languages. They were based on 'pictograms' which are simple drawings representing words such as 'man', 'horse' or 'water'. Gradually more words were added and today a Chinese dictionary may contain as many as 40,000 of these characters.

It is a difficult language to learn and the average educated Chinese person knows between 5,000 and 10,000 characters. To make it easier, about 2,000 of these characters were simplified in 1954.

The geography of China

China's coastline stretches for 6,400 kilometres, running from icy North Korea to the tropical warmth of the South China Sea. To the west, China stretches 3,000 kilometres into the heart of Asia, with agricultural lands, desert, plains and mountains. In the north is the vast Gobi Desert. The most northerly part is Manchuria, rimmed by the border with Russia.

There are three great rivers – the Huang He (Yellow River), the Chiang Jiang (Yangtze) and the Xi Jiang, which forms the Zhu Jiang (Pearl River) near its delta on the coast.

The climate of China is essentially dry in winter and wet in summer.

9

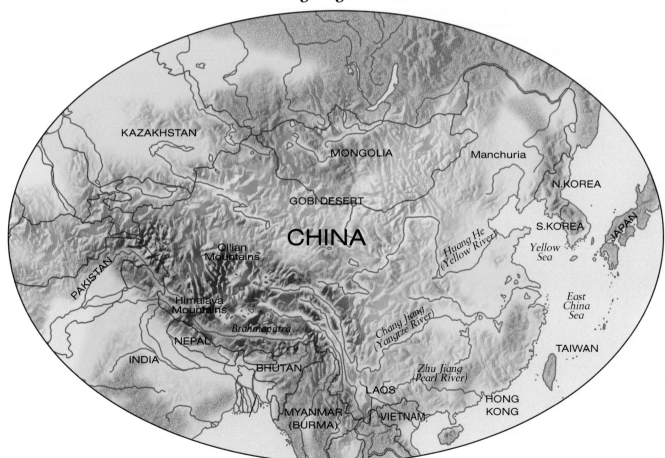

AN ANCIENT CIVILISATION

The Chinese were the first people to make silk, cast iron, paper, fireworks, porcelain and navigational compasses, among other things. When the Italian explorer Marco Polo visited China in 1275–92, he was amazed at what he saw. Because of China's vast size and different cultures, it has always been difficult to hold together as a united nation. This remains a key issue even today.

IMPERIAL CHINA

Qin Shi Huangdi is thought to have been the first emperor (221–210 BC), founding the Qin dynasty. When he died he was buried in a massive tomb in the capital of Xian, surrounded by lifesize pottery soldiers, the so-called 'Terracotta Army'.

Six major dynasties followed – the Han, Tang, Song, Yuan, Ming and Qing. The Chinese emperors were always in fear of invasion and they built an enormous defence barrier – the Great Wall of China.

Confucianism

Life in Imperial China was strongly influenced by a philosophy called Confucianism. This was based on the teachings of Kongfuzi and set out a way of life based on morality, obedience and respect for one's parents and the State.

The Great Wall of China (covering 6,400 km) took centuries to build.

In 1207, Genghis Khan and his Mongolian army stormed over the Great Wall and captured northern China. He created a vast empire and founded the Yuan dynasty.

Ancient Chinese emperors thought they were ordained by the gods to rule. They also believed they were the only civilised people and treated foreigners as barbarians. They did, however, have distant trading links, using a route known as the Silk Roads.

Admiral Zheng He

In 1405, an explorer called Admiral Zheng He (Cheng Ho) reached India and Africa in a series of sailing expeditions. After his death, however, China turned its back on world exploration.

Many of the historic buildings bear the architectural style of China's imperial rulers.

11

The Terracotta Army – one of the world's great archeological treasures

The Opium Wars

To the Chinese Imperial government, opium was evil. To the British, opium was a useful trade commodity. This led to the opium wars in 1839, when China seized 20,000 cases of British opium in Guangzhou.

The barbarians arrive

The Qing (or Manchu) dynasty was the last of the great Chinese dynasties. During a time of rapid expansion of trade in Europe, traders arrived on the coast of China, attracted by the country's unique luxury goods such as porcelain, silk and tea.

However, the Qing emperor was suspicious of foreign traders and refused to deal with them. In the late 18th century China opened up the port of Guangzhou (Canton) to foreign trade. Trading was slow as China did not want what Europe had to offer. It was only when the British started to exploit the opium trade, resulting in a series of wars, that Western traders won a foothold in China.

Japan

Despite the fact that China and Japan are so close, they have never been good neighbours. There were many disputes, but the battle for occupation of China during the Second Sino-Japanese war (1937–45) was the most brutal. Over 20 million Chinese died during the conflict, which left deep scars and an ongoing resentment.

Stories from the Qing dynasty told of successful military campaigns.

In the Second Sino-Japanese War (1937-45), Japan conquered and occupied most of China.

HUMILIATION

Western intrusion on Chinese soil was the start of the 'Century of Humiliation'. Gradually the intruders increased their presence, bit by bit undermining Chinese traditions, customs and beliefs.

The Chinese emperors were also losing their power and prestige. In 1900, a fierce rebellion broke out against foreigners led by a secret martial arts society called the 'Boxers'. It was eventually

The 'Chinese diaspora'

There are large communities of Chinese all over the world. Many live in areas known as 'Chinatowns' in large cities such as London. Large-scale emigration did not begin until the 19th century when Western nations needed cheap labour. Many of these labourers stayed on and opened their own businesses.

suppressed by European, American and Japanese troops, but China was forced to accept trade concessions and pay compensation.

The last emperor of China was an infant boy called Puyi. In 1911, the Qing dynasty was overthrown and China was declared a republic.

Empress Dowager Cixi. In 1898 she imprisoned her own nephew, Emperor Guangxu, to gain power in China.

NATIONALISTS AND COMMUNISTS

In 1919, China was being ruled by warlords who supported the government, and the country was close to civil war. At this time the Republic's first president, Dr Sun Yat-sen, formed a breakaway republic based around his Nationalist Party, the Kuomintang (KMT).

In 1921, inspired by the Russian Communists, the Chinese Communist Party (CCP) was formed. Sun Yat-sen had a short-lived alliance with the party, but when he died in 1925, his place was taken by a far more militant Chiang Kai-shek. Under his control, the KMT massacred many Communists in an attempt to unify China.

Russian Communists showed how power could be given to peasants and workers.

Surviving Communists fled, including Mao Zedong, who later became the Communist leader.

In the 1930s, Japan took advantage of the chaos in China and conquered many of their main cities and ports. When the Japanese were eventually forced out of China, both Nationalists and Communists raced to fill the void. The Communists triumphed and the Nationalists were forced to retreat to the island of Taiwan. The era of Mao's Communist China – renamed the People's Republic of China (PRC) – had well and truly taken hold.

14

The Long March
In October 1934, many Communists were trapped in Jiangxi. 100,000 broke free and travelled more than 9,000 kilometres to Shaanxi. Only about 8,000 survived.

COMMUNIST CHINA

China became a communist country in 1949, and today is the only major country in the world ruled by such a regime. China has seen many changes, particularly under the rule of Mao Zedong. As a direct result of Mao's policies, many millions of Chinese people died, and yet he is still revered even today.

Wherever you go in China, tributes to Mao are never far away.

BEHIND CLOSED DOORS

When Mao Zedong took control in 1949, he had many problems to solve. After decades of war, the Chinese economy was in tatters and the nation was deeply divided. To boost communist power and create stability, Mao started by getting rid of the opposition. Anyone who opposed the new regime was arrested, sent to a labour camp or even worse, killed. Thousands of people died for their beliefs during the first five years of communist rule. This was the era of the Cold War, when China sealed itself off from the rest of the world.

THE GREAT CAMPAIGNS

China's peasants and factory workers had suffered greatly from the unfairness of Imperial China. In principle, they stood to benefit from the new communist government, but this presented an enormous challenge.

To achieve better schools, housing, healthcare, jobs and sufficient food to feed the people, Mao demanded loyalty and discipline from his subjects. Government officers helped to impose a strict regime, under which even school children were expected to chant revolutionary songs at school. All property now belonged to the state and industries were nationalised. The CCP ruled with an iron rod and everyone had to comply.

A major campaign called the 'Great Leap Forward' began in 1957. It was designed to rapidly convert China into a major industrial power. Society was reorganised into huge working communes, and anyone who rebelled was quickly suppressed.

Deng Xiaoping
Deng Xiaoping (1904–97) was a dedicated communist who took part in the Long March in 1934. He rose to power as deputy premier under Zhou Enlai in 1973. Deng's main aims were to push ahead with economic modernisation and to try and improve relations with Western nations. He was a major influence in China and the chief architect of its modernisation. He died at the age of 92.

In the 1970s, Mao agreed to table tennis matches with US teams, helping to improve international relations.

Mao Zedong

Mao Zedong (1893–1976) was a major figure in 20th-century history. He ruled China for almost three decades, witnessing incredible changes. He was adored by millions, not just in China but all over the world. His book *The Thoughts of Chairman Mao* (nicknamed 'The Little Red Book') is the second most printed book after the Bible, with 900 million copies having been produced.

Mao was driven by his vision of a united China, but in his haste to achieve this, he introduced social and economic experiments that proved disastrous. Mao died at the age of 82.

The campaign was a disaster and the result was the greatest man-made famine in history. Some 14–20 million people starved to death.

In 1966, Mao introduced the 'Cultural Revolution' which was intended to shake up Chinese society and eradicate his rivals. The revolution ended in 1969, but the effects lived on and, thanks to a lot of publicity, Mao's status was given a significant boost.

Tienanmen Square is dominated by Mao's tomb – a fitting reminder of the great leader.

17

INTERNATIONAL RELATIONS

At the start of the Cold War, the West was worried that China would form an alliance with the Soviet Union (USSR). Both nations had a close relationship with the Communist regime of North Korea. When China intervened to help North Korea during the Korean War (1950–53), the Western world was not happy. Further conflicts with India and their support of North Vietnam during the overthrow of Pol Pot in the Vietnam War (1959–75), did nothing to improve relations.

To the West's relief, fears of an alliance between China and the USSR proved unfounded. When the Soviet leader, Stalin, died in 1956, the USSR adopted a less rigid form of communism. Mao made it known that he disagreed with this policy and the USSR gradually withdrew its advisers from China. By 1960 the rift was complete.

Tienanmen Square

In the 1980s, Communism across the world came under great pressure. Tensions in China were building up, and it all came to a head on 4 May 1989, when one million students and workers gathered in Tienanmen Square, calling for democratic reform. For a while the government allowed the protest, but on 4 June the army intervened. No one really knows how many protesters were killed – the official number is 200, but the death-toll is suspected to be far higher. Many protesters are in prison, others are still missing.

US president Richard Nixon with Mao Zedong in the 1970s

Nixon in China

The Vietnam War was the US's worst conflict with communism. Over 57,000 Americans and more than 2 million Vietnamese were killed. At the height of the war, President Richard Nixon tried to improve relations with China. Because China had so few contacts with the rest of the world, Nixon had to use unorthodox methods to obtain a meeting – he arranged for the US to play China at table tennis. This was enough to secure a high-level meeting and that same year China agreed to join the United Nations (UN).

Hong Kong

In 1842, as part of the Treaty of Nanking, China was forced to hand over the island of Hong Kong to the British. Hong Kong was turned into a great trading port and, after World War II, into one of the world's leading financial centres. When it was passed back to China in June 1997, many people working in Hong Kong were not happy about the alliance with a communist country. However, the CCP has allowed it some freedom and it continues to thrive financially.

19

FROM MAO TO DENG

When Mao died in 1976, there was a brief power struggle within the CCP. Supporters of the Cultural Revolution tried to cling onto power, but the more moderate Deng Xiaoping won the battle.

Although China had found a way to produce enough food for its citizens, it was still 30 years behind the Western world in terms of technology and the standards of living. Deng knew that if China were to progress, things had to change. His policies allowed a little more freedom, meaning that people had more of a say regarding their own money and jobs. Also, by opening its doors to foreign trade, China forged ahead in the world of commerce and modernisation.

? Can China become a democracy?

When the students called for reform at Tienanmen Square in 1989, the world wondered if China might be on the brink of democracy. Although democracy would bring many advantages, it could also bring chaos. China has a history of highly centralised harsh rule, and it would be hard to make the change.

Perhaps the way forward is for the voice of the people to be heard through their communities, rather than on the basis of one-person, one-vote elections.

In the 1970s, China was 30 years behind the Western world in terms of technology and standards of living.

QUEST FOR DEMOCRACY

Most of the Chinese, especially the young, hoped that China would move towards greater democracy. However, the CCP, which firmly held onto power, had no intentions of making political changes. China still remains a one-party state. The public still do not get a chance to vote.

After the massacre at Tienanmen Square, China's economic and political reforms came to a halt. A new leader emerged in 1993, Jiang Zemin. He reintroduced many reforms and the boom really took off.

By the time of Mao's death, China had recovered from the great famines of the early 1960s.

Many Western influences can now be seen in China, for example, it is not uncommon to see Starbucks and Ikea.

21

WORKSHOP OF THE WORLD

The achievement of China's economic development over the last 25 years has been phenomenal. It produces 33 per cent of the world's computers, 40 per cent of the world's televisions and 66 per cent of microwave ovens. This success story is down to the Chinese society who are driven by a powerful ambition to modernise and get rich at the same time. They want a better world not just for themselves, but for their children as well.

WINNING WAYS

One of China's greatest assets is its enormous (and cheap) workforce. With wages less than US$1 per hour, the cost of manufacturing is kept to a minimum.

Export is big business in China, and two-thirds are now products made for foreign companies. China has also been successful in attracting major foreign companies to set up businesses in their major cities. Special areas called Special Economic Zones (SEZs), with large industrial parks, have been specifically designed for foreign investors.

Fifty per cent of the world's clothes are now made in China.

Technological shift

The foreign companies not only brought jobs for millions of Chinese workers, but they also brought their technological knowledge. China quickly learned how to produce high-quality goods.

Many of the old and inefficient state-owned enterprises have now closed down. China has not turned its back on heavy industry completely, though, and still produces ships, cars and trains. One major project is the Maglev, Shanghai's magnetic-levitation train.

Some 50 million people now live in a cluster of Special Economic Zones, such as Shenzhen (*above*).

Communism and wealth

23

In 2001, the CCP stated it would allow business people to become members of the Party, under a scheme set up by President Jiang Zemin.

It was a clever move. They hoped that by allowing some people to become wealthy, it would lead the way and help those less well-off. Now a quarter of the names on the list of China's richest people are members of the Party.

The Maglev train-link to Shanghai's airport opened in 2004 and reaches speeds of 430 km/h.

NATURAL RESOURCES

To keep up with its rapid growth, China has needed an enormous increase in its natural resources. Luckily China is rich in many of these as the world's leading producer of coal, aluminium and zinc. China supplies one fifth of the world's oil supplies, but it still needs to import a third of what it uses. Its building boom also uses 40 per cent of the world's concrete and 27 per cent of the world's steel. Because of this enormous demand, world prices of steel, copper and oil have risen sharply, which has had a major impact on world markets.

China's oil industry produces one fifth of the world's oil supplies.

24

? **Should Western architects design prestige buildings for the Chinese government?**

In September and October 2004, Beijing hosted an international architecture fair which attracted many of the world's leading architects. China is currently one of the most exciting countries for modern architecture. One example of their innovative design is the National Swimming Centre in Beijing (*right*), designed by an Australian-based company. The rush to design buildings for China has attracted some criticism.

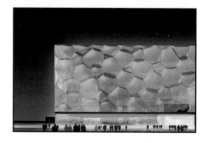

Like many cities in China, the skyline of Shanghai's Pudong financial district is dotted with skyscrapers.

REAPING THE REWARDS

The benefits of China's industrial boom can best be seen in the cities. The skylines of cities such as Shanghai and Guangzhou are dotted with skyscrapers.

Once all property was owned by the State, but today 70 per cent of homes in Shanghai are privately owned. Cars sales have shot up – some 2 million cars were sold in 2003, 80 per cent higher than 2002.

When Mao ruled, all the Chinese people dressed in blue worksuits and rode bicycles. Today, they are fashion conscious and love to go shopping. Leisure has also become big business with many cinemas, internet cafés and bowling alleys. China is reaping the benefits of advancement.

Chinese shopping malls mimic those in the Western world.

The Shanghai International Circuit – host of the first Chinese Grand Prix in 2004 – is now the most challenging Formula 1 track in the world.

26

NATIONAL PRESTIGE

The Chinese government is keen to promote its country as a modern, successful and prosperous state, while maintaining its own identity. It has already attracted a lot of international publicity, with its impressive building projects.

China sees enormous advantages in staging prestigious sporting events, such as the Beijing 2008 Olympics. China also invested a lot of money in its soccer team for the World Cup of 2002. It spent an estimated £133 million on international motor racing when it staged its first ever Grand Prix in Shanghai in 2004. It even hosted the Miss World Contest in 2003 and 2004.

In addition to their sporting achievements, China has also attracted many international music performers. American R&B star Alicia Keys performed at the first foreign concert staged at the Great Wall. Tickets for her concert were the equivalent of three days' pay for many workers.

Of course none of these achievements would have been possible without the support of the Chinese people. All the events mentioned above were well supported. This is probably because for the first time in many years, the Chinese people are able to afford things that they could once only have dreamed about.

STRESSES AND STRAINS

Not everyone in China is benefiting from the economic boom. While the wealthy are concentrated in the coastal cities of the east, the majority of the population live in deprived rural areas inland. They only earn one-third of the city wages. Many workers headed for the cities in search of better wages, only to find the conditions were worse.

PEOPLE ON THE MOVE

Over the past 20 years, over 200 million Chinese have left the country and headed for the cities. Believing they would find work and a better standard of living, many were disappointed. Factory workers can earn as little as £2 a day, working up to 11 hours a day, six days a week.

In an effort to save money to support their families back home, the workers are forced to sleep in meagre dormitories. These workers feel let down by the CCP, aware they are not benefiting from the economic boom.

The attraction of work in the cities led to a mass migration, but the dreams were not always fulfilled.

Urban sprawl

It is not easy for those people who have always lived in the cities. The traditional houses, which created a close sense of community, have been replaced by tower blocks. Many of the old communities have been uprooted and people have to live in modern flats. Most of them feel isolated with no sense of community at all. The areas they once knew have been turned into giant building sites.

The Three Gorges Dam

The CCP is in control of all major developments in China. Some are vast, such as the Three Gorges Dam on the Yangtze River. This is the world's largest engineering project and will be the world's biggest hydroelectric power station. It is designed to prevent the floods that have caused devastation.

Strains on the system

One of the main ambitions of the Chinese now is to own a car. If the figure reaches those of the US (two cars to every household), there could be over 650 million cars in China. This is more than the rest of the world put together! This is starting to put strains on the already busy roads. China is desperately trying to build new roads, but the problem of pollution is becoming a big concern.

This project, due to be completed in 2011, has caused much controversy. The Three Gorges, once a scenic stretch of river, is now dominated by a 641-kilometre-long reservoir. Environmentalists fear that this massive dam could alter the climate in the region.

At present China's roads, railways, aircraft, ships, communication systems and power supplies are inadequate to meet the country's needs. The economic boom has made the situation even worse. Cities frequently suffer from power cuts and China is now looking at alternatives such as hydroelectric power. They are hoping that the Three Gorges Dam (*see page 28*) will help solve some of their problems.

With no state-run farms, farmers now work under contract.

Crisis in the countryside

Farming is a vital part of China's economy, not only in exports but to provide food for the Chinese population. However, due to high tax demands, the farmers are feeling frustrated and angry as they are finding it harder and harder to make a living. This frustration has triggered a series of violent riots.

Is China's growth set to continue?

- If global demand slows down it could affect China's economy.
- China's economy could produce more than the market can absorb.
- If growth rate cannot be sustained, it may cause social conflict.
- China's banks may not be able to pay back their massive loans.

- Foreign countries could introduce import taxes to curb competition.
- Demands for democracy could end up in political turmoil.
- If labour costs rise, foreign businesses may look elsewhere.
- Despite China's efforts to modernise, foreign companies have come across corruption and piracy.

DEAF EARS

One of the problems with the Chinese political system is that there is no one to complain to. Rather than listen to the people who work for them, the government tends to concentrate on protecting their own businesses and profits. The only way an ordinary person can hope to get noticed is to disguise his complaint as a constructive suggestion for change. They can join official pressure groups or non-governmental organisations (NGOs), but very often the CCP will not tolerate such groups and closes them down without warning.

CENSORSHIP

The CCP has three ways of keeping criticism at bay: censorship, propaganda and suppression. The government controls all the media and stops the publishing or broadcasting of any information that could be harmful to the State. It also censors use of the internet, jokingly referred to as the 'Great Firewall of China'.

Commercial radio stations offer a wide range of subject matter, but when it comes to news items they mustn't rock the boat!

Strangers in their own land

Workers that have emigrated from rural areas into the cities in search of work, say they feel like strangers in their own country. They do not have the same rights as native city-dwellers – such as education, pensions or welfare. To qualify for permanent status, a worker needs to have lived in the city for seven years.

Many migrant workers have been driven to suicide by appalling conditions and low wages.

Burying the truth

Because the government has total control over the media, it is able to portray its country in the best possible light. This also means that it can hide uncomfortable truths. For example, China is facing an AIDS crisis – it is estimated it will have ten million victims by 2010.

If the government feels that someone has expressed unfair dissent, they can act brutally. The offender may be arrested and forced to spend many years in prison. The CCP also has strict methods of dealing with crime. It is believed that as many as 700 people are executed every year, many of them in public.

Minorities and dissidents

The Chinese government has been strongly criticised for its treatment of minority groups. Although Chinese culture is a mixture of many faiths, the government does not encourage any religion. It has tried to limit outside influences and has a strong dislike for the religious sect Falun Gong ('Buddhist Law'), which encourages meditation. The government went as far as banning the sect altogether. They have also been criticised for their treatment of Tibetans, a group which makes up about 8 per cent of the population.

31

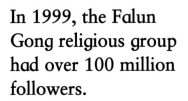
In 1999, the Falun Gong religious group had over 100 million followers.

FEELING LET DOWN

Many workers in China feel disillusioned by the CCP and the treatment they receive. In the past, state-run industries provided them with work, pensions, healthcare and even a home. Today, despite the freedom from repression, the ordinary person does not feel their needs are being met.

Many people are leaving China in an effort to lift themselves out of poverty. They are even prepared to put themselves in the hands of illegal traffickers. Instead of a better life, these people have been open to exploitation and some have even died as a result.

The SARS crisis

SARS (Severe Acute Respiratory Syndrome) is a new killer disease that began in southern China in 2002. Because the government tried to cover up the outbreak, the disease spread. It wasn't until 2003 that they faced up to the problem and informed the World Health Organisation. By June 2003, 775 people had died and thousands more were affected. The SARS crisis hit the Chinese tourist industry hard, and was a lesson well learned. It proved that China's tendency to secrecy could be detrimental to its reputation and economy.

32

PUTTING UP WITH IT

Despite their many doubts, Chinese people still have great hopes for the future. Those who are enjoying the benefits of the boom say it is all down to their leaders. Although the CCP may be secretive and have some strict policies, in general Chinese people feel freer to express their opinions than ever before. There is no doubt it is more flexible than in the past.

Brothers and sisters have I none

By the 1970s, China's already huge population was spiralling out of control. Aware that there soon would not be enough food to go around, the government introduced a law in 1979, stating that married couples could only have one child. This had many adverse side-effects. There are now more boys than girls in China. Children are under unbearable pressure to succeed in school. Parents have less offspring to support them in old age and children are showing signs of selfishness.

The environment

Of the 20 most polluted cities in the world, 16 are in China. The reasons are:

• 80 per cent of China's electricity is generated by burning high-sulphur coal.

• All major rivers, a source of drinking water, are dangerously polluted by sewage and industrial waste.

• Deforestation has caused massive soil erosion and flooding.

The good news is that China is working on all these problems.

33

INTERNATIONAL RELATIONS

Now that China is in touch with the rest of the world, its activities are of global importance. Once treated with some caution, China is now keen to cement international relations. China cannot afford to upset countries with whom it trades, and yet it wishes to maintain its own unique customs and traditions.

Chinese president Hu Jintao at the Asia-Pacific Economic Co-operation Summit in Santiago, Chile.

The question of Taiwan
Taiwan is an island located 150 kilometres off the coast of China (the PRC). The PRC has always maintained that Taiwan is their territory. If Taiwan ever declares its independence, it could provoke China into invading. Hopefully, Taiwan and China will soon be able to see eye to eye, encouraging a possible reunification.

REGIONAL POLITICS
China's prime concerns are its direct neighbours – Japan, South Korea and Taiwan. All are important trading links, and China's recent successful dealings with Japan have helped to smooth over the scars left by previous conflicts in the 20th century.

China also has mutually profitable relations with the Association of South-East Asian Nations (ASEAN), which brings together ten nations. In 2001, China, Japan and Korea formed a link with ASEAN, forming ASEAN + 3.

China's relationship with North Korea is not so stable. It is a staunchly communist country dominated by its leader Kim Jong II. North Korea is suspicious of China because of its diplomatic relations with South Korea, their sworn enemy.

China believes that Taiwan belongs to them and on several occasions has threatened to invade. This has become an important factor in international relations and for that reason it is important that the two countries learn to coexist and stop further conflicts.

The Chinese army—the People's Liberation Army (PLA)—is essentially the Communist Party's army. The majority of soldiers are rural peasants.

Should the international community make an issue of China's human rights record?

The world was outraged when they heard about the Tienanmen Square massacre. Many countries vowed not to deal with China while it treated its citizens so badly. Since then, however, China's human rights record has not improved, but its booming economy has encouraged the world to turn a blind eye.

The Chinese government is very sensitive about any form of criticism. Hopefully by continuing to trade with China, the rest of the world can teach them democracy.

SUPERPOWER ACROSS THE SEA

China's relationship with the US is quite complicated. During the Cold War, the US formed a basic understanding with China to try and put pressure on the Soviet Union. Since 1978, the US has become China's largest trading partner.

Because the US dollar is the main world currency, China is buying many US government bonds. This has the effect of supporting the US's huge trade deficit, which many believe to be a dangerous situation. This means the US economy is now reliant on China.

Since the 1970s, when President Nixon began to open diplomatic discussions with China, relations between the two countries have grown stronger.

China is worried that the value of the dollar could drop, making their investments less valuable.

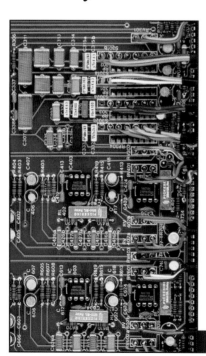

Many US computer companies have invested in China, taking advantage of their technical talents.

Although the two countries are linked financially, with regards to politics they are worlds apart. Neither country wants any confrontation, and China is keen to show its support in the US's fight against terrorism and nuclear weapons. Trading agreements between the US, Japan and China have formed a formidable triangle.

OTHER PLAYERS

Although relations between China and Russia have been sticky in the past, in recent years the rift seems to have been closing. In 2001, they both signed a friendship and co-operation treaty.

China has found Russia to be a good source for weapons and military technology. Russia could also play a vital role in the future, supplying much needed oil for China's ever expanding industries.

Relations with Russia may improve through the export of oil to China.

The European Union (EU) is a major market for Chinese goods, and China is a source of low-cost manufacturing for the EU.

Can Japan and China bury the hatchet?

Past military intervention by Japan during the 20th century has left a sour taste in the mouths of many Chinese. Since then Japan has invested heavily in China and in return China has granted them many trading concessions. Japan has also donated aid to help improve their roads and railways. China provides a valuable market for Japan, taking 48 per cent of its exports. The two countries definitely have many mutual interests and, as tourist traffic continually increases between Japan and China, it appears they can bury the hatchet.

A delegation from the People's Republic of China at the UN in 1971.

UN Secretary-General Kofi Annan meets Wang Guangya.

THE WORLD STAGE

China's key position in world economy is increasingly obvious. China joined the United Nations (UN) in 1971, and is one of the five permanent members of its Security Council. With the support of the US, the EU and Japan, China joined the World Trade Organisation in 2001, alongside Taiwan.

China is not currently a member of G-8, which represents the world's top industrial nations. It has been invited as an observer and is likely to receive an offer of membership soon. It is already a member of the G-20, which contains the G-8 countries, plus 12 other important industrialised nations. Among these are India and Brazil, both of whom have close relations with China.

Together, China, India and Brazil made a stand at the World Trade Organisation's meeting in Mexico in 2003, asking for a better deal for developing countries.

THE NEW SUPERPOWER?

Since the collapse of the Soviet Union, there is only one real superpower in the world – the US. It has the largest economy and the most powerful military force. It also has a lifestyle and culture that many people envy. However, history shows no superpower lasts forever; there is always someone waiting to challenge it.

Perhaps China could be the one to do it.

If China can maintain its development, it is set to play a leading role in the global economy for many years.

INDUSTRIAL BASE

By offering low-cost manufacturing to the world on a scale that has never been matched, China has become a formidable contender for the title of 'superpower'. Added to this, it has proved that it has the technical knowledge to advance further. Could China become the world's largest economy by 2020?

What constitutes a superpower?

• Economic strength and global reach in trade.
• Military strength.
• Geographical size and population.
• Global cultural influence.
• A desire to be a world leader.

MILITARY STRENGTH

China not only has the world's largest army, it also has nuclear weapons. At present most of its military equipment is said to be about 20 years out of date, but that is set to change.

As China becomes more wealthy, it is investing in more sophisticated weapons, ships and aircraft, mainly with the help of Russia.

At present it has no need for advanced technical weapons. Its main military concerns at the moment are defence of its borders, controlling civil disobedience and protecting itself from a possible future nuclear attack.

China has the world's largest army.

The Chinese space programme

China became the third nation to put a man in space in 2003. The astronaut was Yang Yiwei. In autumn 2008, the first spacewalk by a Chinese astronaut took place. Future plans in their space programme include other manned flights, a large space

telescope, exploration of the Moon, a space station served by a space shuttle and space tourism. Although the costs are huge, China wishes to show to the world what it is capable of achieving in space technology.

AMBITION

In general China does not want to meddle in other nations' affairs and expects to be treated in the same way. When it has tried to intervene in the past with some of its neighbours – Vietnam, Cambodia, Laos and Indonesia – these ventures proved short-lived and unsatisfactory. China's main ambition is to concentrate on its own policies and the well-being of its thriving country.

China's history suggests that it would not want to be a global power as it is not an aggressive nation.

Superpower or not?

This leads us to the question: does China really want to become a superpower? It would seem at present they only want to concentrate on putting their own problems in order. If you ask the question in China, it is generally met with disbelief. Perhaps China is being portrayed as a possible superpower because other countries believe they are a genuine threat. This might explain why the US is taking an aggressive stance to protect its own superpower status.

The rise of the Chinese economy: who wins, who loses?

Did you know that China is the world's largest producer of garlic? Because China can keep costs low, many industries around the world have been decimated by the arrival of cheap Chinese produce / goods.

Other companies have taken advantage of the low Chinese labour costs – such as Nike, Timberland, Kodak and General Motors – boosting their own profits. Brazil has also profited from China's need for iron ore, steel, leather and soybeans.

41

Russian prime minister Vladimir Putin (left) and Indian prime minister Manmohan Singh

OTHER CONTENDERS

If China does not wish to become a superpower, then there are other countries who might. For example, the European Union (EU) certainly has the size and economic strength. However, the belief of the EU is to promote peace rather than the projection of power.

Russia was a superpower until the collapse of communism in 1990. It still hopes to recover this status.

India, the second largest nation on Earth, has many parallels with China, but has never shown any ambition to become a superpower.

42

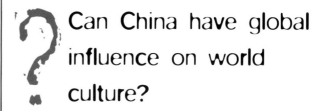

Can China have global influence on world culture?

One aspect of America's superpower status is its cultural impact on the rest of the world. Can China ever match that?

Chinese culture is spreading quickly and we can see evidence of it wherever we look – in food, silk, martial arts such as tai chi, sporting prowess, herbal medicine, acupuncture and many more areas besides.

A DIFFERENT ANALYSIS

It is possible that the concept of being a superpower is now outdated and that there are no new candidates. It is suggested that the world will be divided into three power centres – something called 'tri-regionalism'. One region would be the US (united with all the countries in the Americas). Another would be the EU (possibly in conjuction with Russia). The third would be East Asia (possibly in conjunction with China and India). Having said that, China will no doubt stay a powerful country and a major player on the world stage.

Weapons of mass destruction

China tested its first atomic bomb in 1964 and an H-bomb in 1967. Although it is known to have built up a healthy nuclear arsenal, like many other major nations it signed the Nuclear Non-Proliferation Treaty in 1968. China says it is committed to reducing its nuclear stockpiles and has denied that it has any biological or chemical weapons.

China has come a long way since the days of imperial rule.

43

CHRONOLOGY

1368 – The Ming dynasty began (1368–1644).

1644 – The Qing dynasty, China's last imperial dynasty (1644–1912), was founded.

1839 – The First Opium War broke out.

1895 – China had lost Korea, Taiwan and a part of Manchuria to the Japanese at the end of the First Sino-Japanese War.

1911 – The last emperor, 5-year-old boy Puyi, was overthrown by republican revolutionaries.

1921 – The Chinese Communist Party (CCP) was founded.

1934 – The communist 'Red Army' escaped KMT forces in Jiangxi Province and began the 'Long March'.

1937 – Start of the Second Sino-Japanese War, with the invasion of China by the Japanese.

1945 – Communists and Nationalists resumed their civil war for control of China.

1949 – The Communists won the civil war. On 1 October, the People's Republic of China was proclaimed, with Mao Zedong as head of state.

1957 – Mao launched the 'Great Leap Forward'.

1959 – Dalai Lama fled to India, following a revolt in Chinese-occupied Tibet.

1964 – China tested its first atomic bomb.

1966 – Mao launched the 'Cultural Revolution'.

1971 – China joined the United Nations.

1972 – US President Nixon was the first president to visit China. He held meetings with Mao Zedong and prime minister Zhou Enlai.

1976 – Mao died at the age of 82.

1978 – The start of China's rapid economic development.

1979 – The first Special Economic Zones (SEZs) were set up to encourage foreign investment.

1989 – Student protestors massacred at Tienanmen Square on 4 June.

1993 – Jiang Zemin became president and announced the resumption of economic reforms.

1997 – China regained Hong Kong from the British.

1999 – Falun Gong religious sect banned after a meeting was broken up in Beijing.

2001 – President Jiang Zemin announced his 'Three Represents' policy. This enabled business people to join the CCP for the first time. China joined the World Trade Organisation.

2002 – Severe outbreak of SARS caused major damage to China's economy and tourism.

2003 – China launched its first manned space mission. Jiang Zemin stepped down as president and was replaced by Hu Jintao.

2004 – China hosted a number of high-profile international events, including the first Shanghai Grand Prix.

2004 – The Maglev, Shanghai's magnetic-levitation train, was launched.

2008 – Beijing hosted the Olympic Games. China's first spacewalk.

45

ORGANISATIONS AND GLOSSARY

Association of South-East Asian Nations (ASEAN) – Founded in 1967 to promote economic growth and peace.

Authoritarian – Demanding obedience.

Capitalist – A society or person that uses money or property to make a profit.

Collective farm – Agricultural land taken over by the State.

Communism – A system of government to remove the inequalities of society.

Consumer society – A saying that emerged in the 1960s to describe people in well-off capitalist countries who love to go shopping.

Dissent – Disagreeing with the majority viewpoint.

Dissident – A persistent critic.

Domestic market – All the buyers and traders in one's own country.

Dynasty – A family of rulers whose power is passed down from one generation to the next.

European Union (EU) – The EU now has 27 member countries.

Free market – Trade that is not regulated by a government.

Government bonds – Certificates people can buy as an investment.

Group of Eight (G-8) – Eight of the world's leading industrial nations who meet regularly for discussions.

Human rights – A broad term used to refer to the essential rights or freedom of any individual.

Imperial – The adjective used in relation to an empire or emperor.

Infrastructure – All the systems used to move people, goods and information around a country (e.g. electricity, road, rail).

International Monetary Fund (IMF) – An agency of the United Nations.

North Atlantic Treaty Organisation (NATO) – Defence organisation founded in 1949.

Political prisoner – A person held for their political beliefs.

Protectionism – A variety of measures used to protect industry from foreign competition.

Republic – A country that is ruled by the people.

Sanctions – A way of showing displeasure when a country has misbehaved.

Sino- – A prefix meaning Chinese.

Slump – A large downturn in the economy of a country, a region or the world.

Special Economic Zones (SEZs) – Industrial zones especially established in major cities to encourage foreign investors.

Totalitarian – Used to describe a government that wants to have total control of everything.

Treaty ports – The set of ports in China where foreign merchants could operate under their own laws and taxation systems.

United Nations (UN) – An international organisation founded in 1945 to promote peace, security and economic development.

World Trade Organisation (WTO) – Established in 1995, with 145 countries as members.

47

INDEX

48

Photo Credits:
Abbreviations: l-left, r-right, b-bottom, t-top, c-centre, m-middle. Front cover main, ml, c and back cover t, 7tl, 7bl, 7br, 11mr, 15tr, 19br, 25bl, 33br – Flat Earth. Front cover mr, 8bl, 21 tr, 28mr, 28bl, 35mr – George Michael. 1ml, 8ml, 14tr, 15ml, 20br, 27mr, 38tl, 41tr, 44tr – Corel. 1c, 40bl – Christopher Lowden. 1mr, 9tr, 9trm, 9trb, 21m, 21b, 23bl, 45bl – Jian Shuo Wang. 2-3b, 3tr, 10br, 11bl, 17br, 23tr, 25tl – Select Pictures. 2bl, 2ml, 4tr, 22bl, 43br – Affordable Stock Photography. 4bl, 5br, 8tr, 29tr, 39mr, 42br – ©Dennis Cox/ChinaStock. 7m, 13mr – PBD. 12bl, 14bm, 44bl – www.informationwar.org. 12br, 13bl – ©ChinaStock. 16bl – ©Wu Yinxian/ChinaStock. 17tl – ©Lu Houmin/ChinaStock. 18bl – AP/Wide World Photos. 19tl, 19ml – US National Archive and Records Administration. 24tr, 33mr – Photodisc. 24 mr, 24br, 45 tr – Arup. 26tl – ©Liu Liqun/ChinaStock. 30br – Gilles Sabrie / WorldPictureNews. 31br – Courtesy of the Falun Dafa Information Center. 32tc – Myles Chilton / WorldPictureNews. 34ml – Josh Stephenson / WorldPictureNews. 36tr – Paul Morse/ www.whitehouse.gov. 36mr – Eric Draper/www.whitehouse.gov. 36bl – Ingram Publishing. 37tr – epa photo / AFI / Normunds Mezins. 38mr – UN Photo / WorldPictureNews. 40mr – Corbis. 42tl – Amit Kumar / WorldPictureNews.